CW00498583

GRADE FOUR

Electric Guitar Playing

compiled by

Tony Skinner

on behalf of

RGT®

Registry of Guitar Tutors

A CIP record for this publication is available from the British Library

ISBN 1-898466-54-8

Published in Great Britain by

REGISTRY PUBLICATIONS LTD

Registry Mews, 11 to 13 Wilton Road, Bexhill, Sussex, TN40 1HY

Music and text typesetting by

Take Note Publishing Limited

54 Lincolns Mead, Lingfield, Surrey RH7 6TA

Printed and bound in Great Britain

Contents

Introduction

This handbook is primarily intended to give advice and information to candidates considering taking the Grade Four examination in electric guitar playing, although undoubtedly it will be found that the information contained within will be helpful to all guitarists whether intending to take the examination or not.

GUITAROGRAPH

In order that scales, arpeggios and chords can be illustrated as clearly as possible, and made available for all to understand regardless of experience, notation and fingering are displayed via the use of the *guitarograph*.

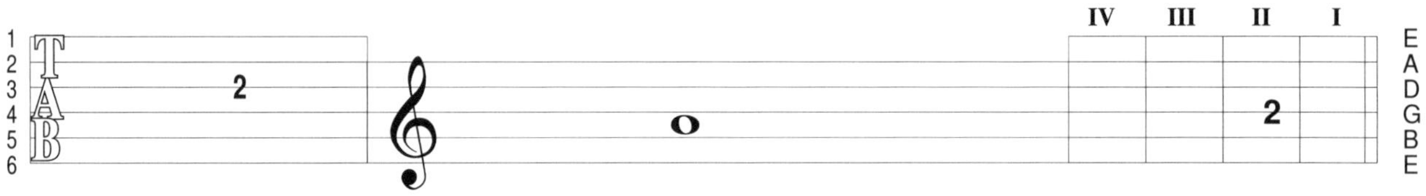

The *guitarograph* uses a combination of tablature, traditional notation and fingerboard diagram – thereby ensuring clarity and leaving no doubt as to what is required. In the example shown above, all three notations refer to the same note, i.e. A on the 2nd fret of the 3rd (G) string, fretted with the 2nd finger. Each of the notation methods used in the *guitarograph* is explained below:

Tablature

The tablature is shown on the left of the guitarograph, with horizontal lines representing the strings (with the high E string being string 1), and the numbers on the string lines referring to the frets. A '0' on a line would mean play that string *open* (unfretted).

This means play at the second fret on the third string.

Musical notation

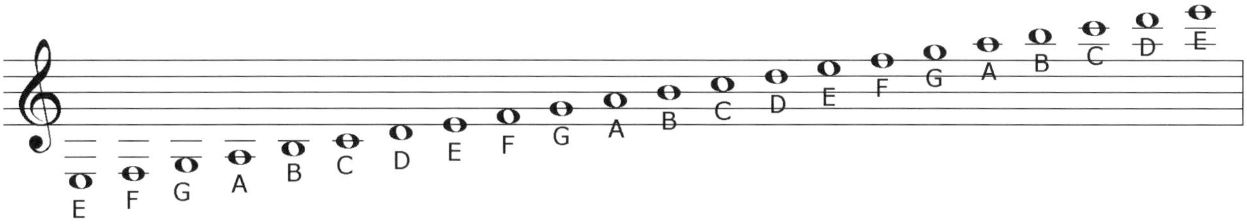

Notation on the treble clef is shown in the centre of the guitarograph.

A sharp (♯) before a note would raise its pitch by a semitone i.e. one fret higher, whilst a flat (♭) before a note would lower the pitch by a semitone, i.e. one fret lower. A natural sign (♮) before a note cancels a sharp or flat sign.

Fingerboard diagram

The fingerboard diagram is shown on the right of the guitarograph with horizontal lines representing the strings. Vertical lines represent the frets, with fret numbers shown in Roman numerals. The numbers on the horizontal lines show the recommended fingering. Fingerings have been chosen which are likely to be the most effective for the widest range of players at this level, however there are a variety of alternative fingerings and fingerboard positions that could be used and you can use any other systematic fingerings that produce a good musical result.

This means play with the second finger at the second fret on the G string.

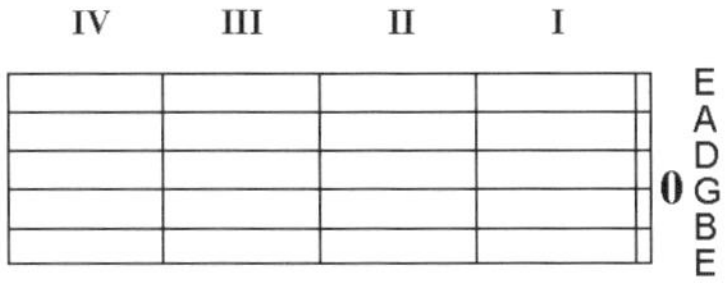

This means play the G string *open*, i.e. without fretting it.

Interval spellings

Above each guitarograph is an interval spelling. This lists the letter names of the notes within the scale, arpeggio or chord, together with their interval numbers. The interval numbers shown are based on their comparison to the major scale with the same starting pitch. The scale, arpeggio and chord spellings will help you identify the differences in construction between the various scales and chords, and will help you learn the names of the notes that you are playing.

For example:

A major scale

A	B	C♯	D	E	F♯	G♯	A
1	2	3	4	5	6	7	8

A natural minor scale

A	B	C	D	E	F	G	A
1	2	♭3	4	5	♭6	♭7	8

ALTERNATIVE FINGERING

Whilst the notes indicated in the guitarographs are precise and definitive, the fingering given in all cases is only one possible recommended suggestion: any alternative systematic and effective fingerings will be acceptable. There is no requirement to use the exact fingerings shown within this book.

TUNING

The use of an electronic tuner or other tuning aid, *prior to, or at the start of the examination*, is permitted; candidates should be able to make any further adjustments, if required during the examination, unaided. The examiner will, upon request, offer an E or A note to tune to.

For examination purposes guitars should be tuned to Standard Concert Pitch (A=440Hz).

Candidates who normally tune to non-standard pitch (e.g. A=442Hz) should revert to Standard Concert Pitch for examination purposes. Candidates who normally tune a full tone or semitone higher/lower should either revert to Standard Pitch for the examination or should be prepared to transpose immediately upon request all requirements to Standard Pitch.

Scales and arpeggios

At this grade candidates should be able to play, in two different fingerboard positions, the following two octave scales in *any* key:

- major
- pentatonic major
- blues
- natural minor

In addition, candidates should be able to play, in one fingerboard position, the following two octave arpeggios starting from *any* note:

- minor 7th
- dominant 7th
- major 7th

Below are examples of the scales and arpeggios required for the Grade Four examination, all illustrated with a starting note of A. All these utilise transpositional finger patterns, so each shape can be moved up or down the fingerboard to a new pitch without the need for a change of fingering. The table below lists the frets on the sixth string that could be used to start each scale and arpeggio, depending upon the pitch required.

F	F♯/G♭	G	G♯/A♭	A	A♯/B♭	B	C	C♯/D♭	D	D♯/E♭	E
1 or 13	2 or 14	3 or 15	4 or 16	5	6	7	8	9	10	11	12

Scales

A MAJOR SCALE – 2 OCTAVES (two different fingerboard positions)

A	B	C♯	D	E	F♯	G♯	A
1	2	3	4	5	6	7	8

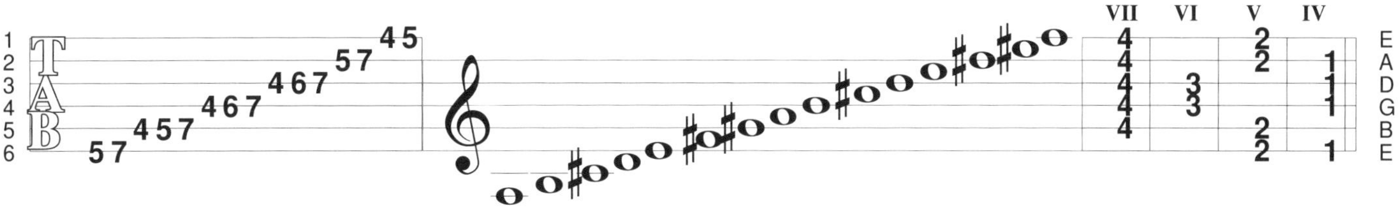

A PENTATONIC MAJOR SCALE – 2 OCTAVES (two different fingerboard positions)

A B C♯ E F♯ A
1 2 3 5 6 8

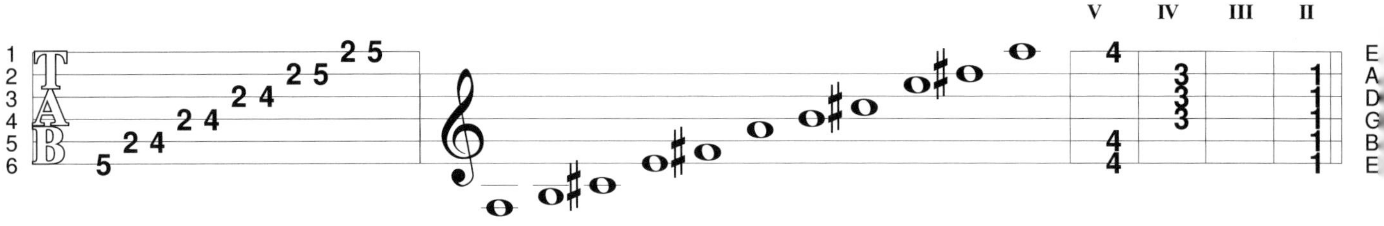

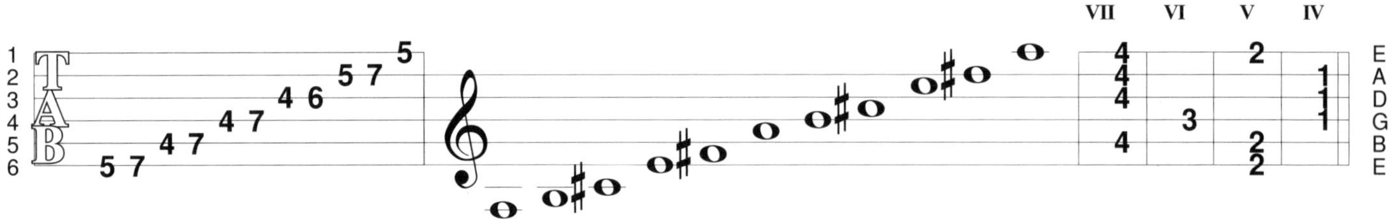

A BLUES SCALE – 2 OCTAVES (two different fingerboard positions)

A C D E♭ E G A
1 ♭3 4 ♭5 5 ♭7 8

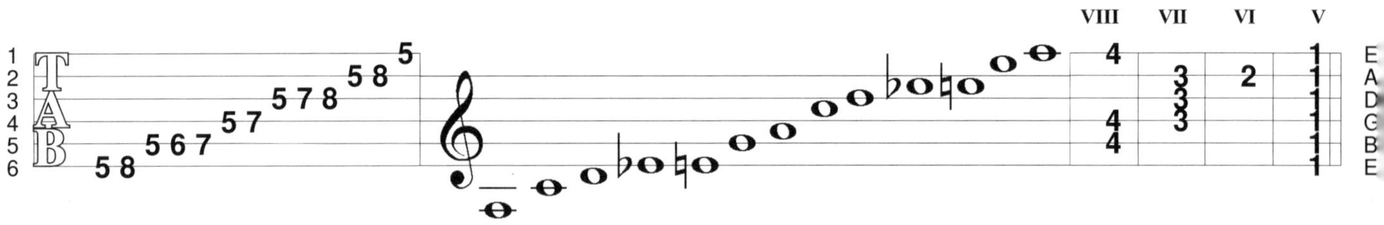

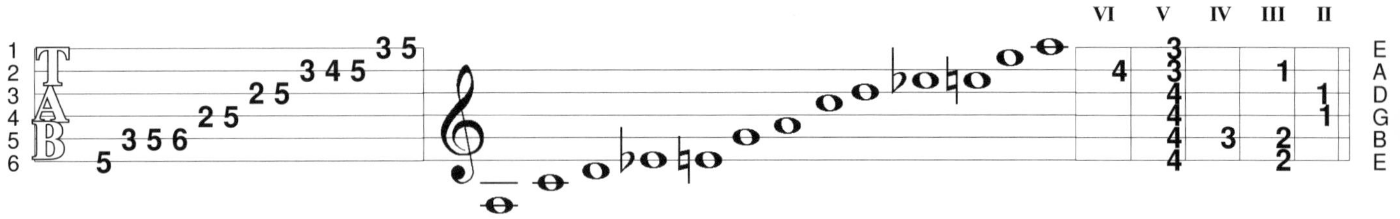

A NATURAL MINOR SCALE – 2 OCTAVES (two different fingerboard positions)

A B C D E F G A
1 2 ♭3 4 5 ♭6 ♭7 8

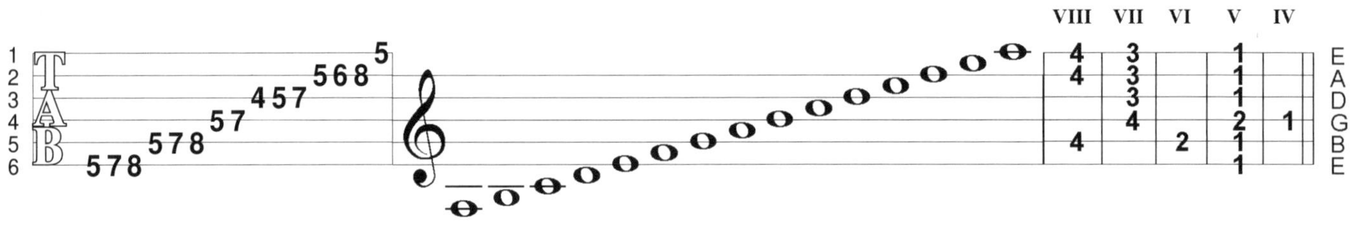

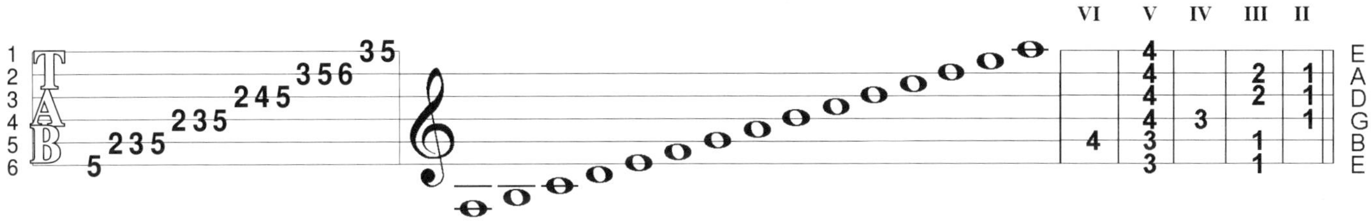

Arpeggios

A MINOR 7TH ARPEGGIO – 2 OCTAVES

A C E G A
1 ♭3 5 ♭7 8

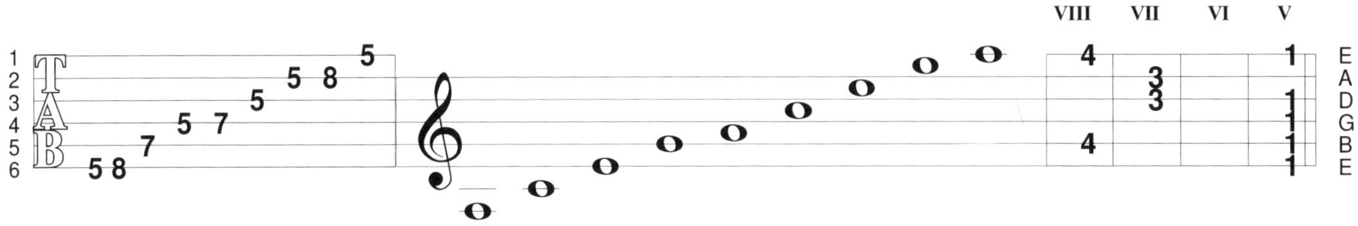

A DOMINANT 7TH ARPEGGIO – 2 OCTAVES

A C♯ E G A
1 3 5 ♭7 8

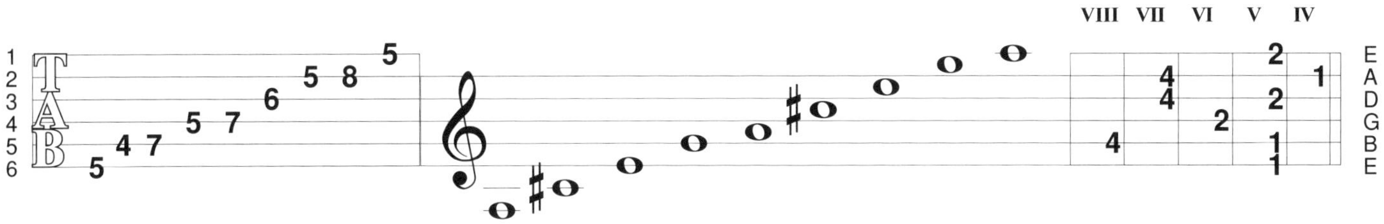

A MAJOR 7TH ARPEGGIO – 2 OCTAVES

A C♯ E G♯ A
1 3 5 7 8

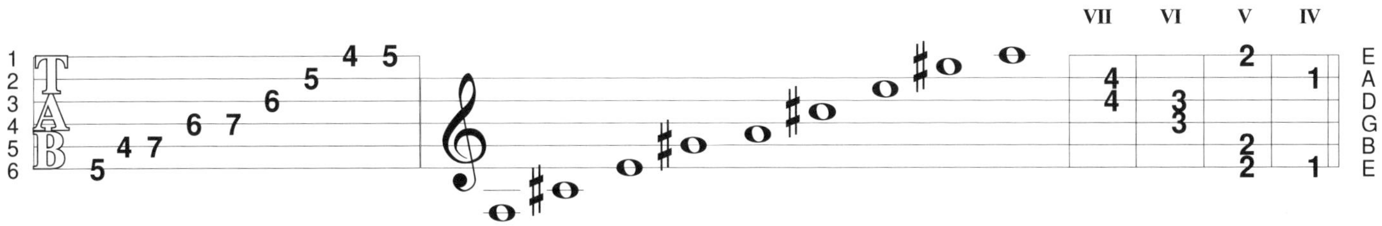

INFORMATION AND ADVICE

A maximum of 12 marks may be awarded in the 'scales' section of the examination.

The examiner may request you to play, from memory, any of the required scales and arpeggios. Each should be played once only, ascending and descending (i.e. from the lowest note to the highest and back again) without a pause and without repeating the top note. Candidates, particularly those using acoustic guitars, will not be asked to play in fingerboard positions that are inaccessible for their particular instrument.

The examiner will request the scales to be demonstrated in two different fingerboard positions. These do not necessarily have to be the positions illustrated in this book: other systematic and effective fingerings may be acceptable, providing the scales are played accurately over the correct range – with both positions played in the same octave.

As a guideline, scales should be played at a tempo of approximately 100 beats per minute (two notes per beat), with arpeggios a little slower at approximately 76 bpm. Choose a tempo at which you feel confident and comfortable and try to maintain this evenly throughout; evenness and clarity are more important than speed for its own sake.

Fretting-hand technique

Press the tips of the fretting-hand fingers as close to the fretwire as possible. This minimises buzzes and the amount of pressure required – enabling you to play with a lighter, clearer and hence more fluent touch.

Try to keep all the fretting-hand fingers close to the fingerboard, and have them ready to press in a 'hovering position', as this minimises the amount of movement required. Always have the fretting hand spread, with the fingers correctly spaced and ready in position hovering, before you start to play.

Picking-hand technique

Although it is not essential to use a plectrum (or pick) for this examination, you may find that not using one has a detrimental effect on speed, attack, volume and tone – or at least more effort will be required to achieve the same effect. However, the use of the fingers, rather than the plectrum, does offer greater flexibility. Ultimately the choice is personal. Both methods are acceptable, providing a strong clear tone is achieved.

If using a plectrum alternate between downstrokes and upstrokes. Grip the plectrum between the index finger and thumb. Position the plectrum so that its tip is just beyond the fingertip. If an excessive amount of plectrum tip extends beyond the finger a lack of pick control will result as the plectrum will flap around when striking the strings – this would consequently reduce fluency and accuracy. Be careful not to grip the plectrum too tightly as excessive gripping pressure can lead to muscular tension in the hand with subsequent loss of flexibility and movement.

Chords

At this grade, candidates should be able to play the following chords at any pitch, using *barre chord shapes*, in *two* different fingerboard positions:

- minor 7th
- dominant 7th
- major 7th
- major
- minor

(Note: major and minor chords have been fully covered in the Grade Three book)

The barre chords below are illustrated with a root note of C, however, because they utilise transpositional shapes they can be moved up or down the fingerboard to any pitch without the need to change fingering.

This table lists the fret position needed to produce chords at different pitches.

First finger on fret number:	1	2	3	4	5	6	7	8	9	10	11	12
Chords with root on E string:	F	F♯/G♭	G	G♯/A♭	A	A♯/B♭	B	C	C♯/D♭	D	D♯/E♭	E
Chords with root on A string:	A♯/B♭	B	C	C♯/D♭	D	D♯/E♭	E	F	F♯/G♭	G	G♯/A♭	A

C minor 7th (root on E string)

C E♭ G B♭

1 ♭3 5 ♭7

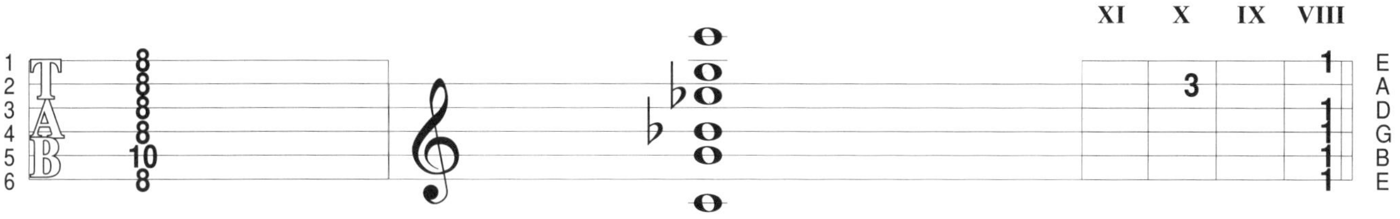

C minor 7th (root on A string)

C E♭ G B♭

1 ♭3 5 ♭7

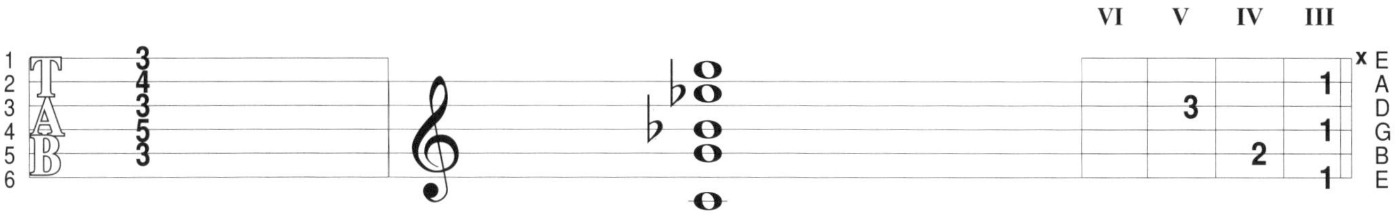

C dominant 7th (root on E string)

C E G B♭

1 3 5 ♭7

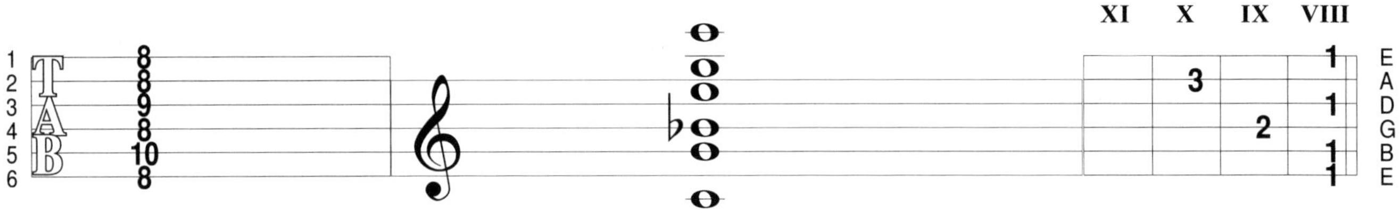

C dominant 7th (root on A string)

C E G B♭

1 3 5 ♭7

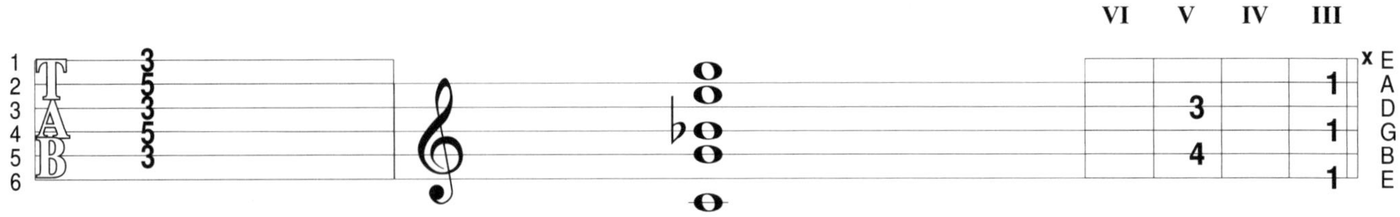

C major 7th (root on E string)

C E G B

1 3 5 7

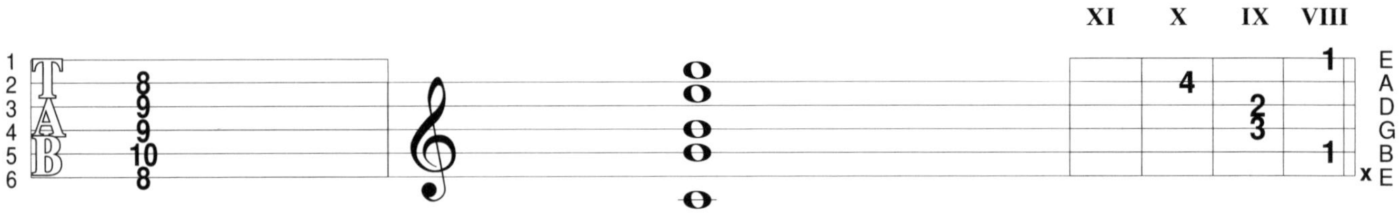

C major 7th (root on A string)

C E G B

1 3 5 7

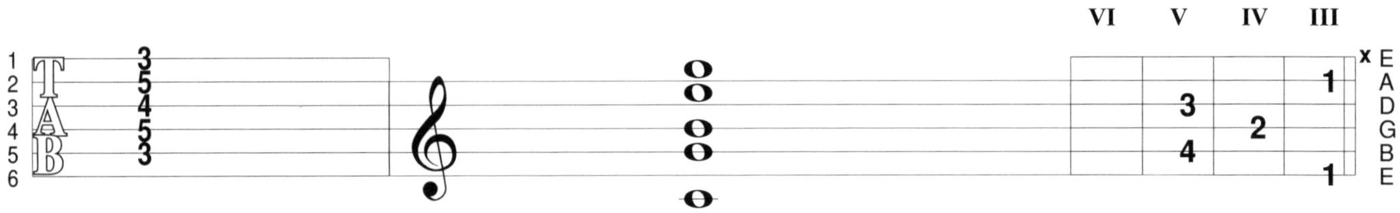

INFORMATION AND ADVICE

A maximum of 8 marks may be awarded in this section of the examination.

The examiner may request you to play, from memory, any of the required chords in two different fingerboard positions. Each chord shape should be played once only, using a single downstroke. Make sure that your fingers are carefully and correctly positioned before playing the chord. In the fingerboard diagrams, strings that should be omitted are marked by an X – so be careful not to strike these strings when playing the chord.

BARRE CHORDS

At this grade, 'barre' chords are used – where the first finger effectively replaces the nut and acts as a 'bar' across all strings. In chords with the root note on the fifth string, although you can still place the first finger barre over all six strings, you are advised to omit the sixth string in your strum.

To ensure that your barre chords ring clearly you should observe the following advice :

(i) The first finger should be straight and in-line with the fret, rather than at an angle to it.

(ii) The first finger need not be completely flat: it can be tilted very slightly away from the fret toward its outer side.

(iii) Position the first finger so that the creases at its joints do not coincide with the strings. If necessary, adjust the barre until you find the optimum position.

(iv) All fingers should be positioned as close to the frets as possible.

(v) Do not exert excessive pressure with either the first finger or the thumb.

(vi) Ensure that fretting fingers, other than the first finger, remain upright and press against the strings with their tips.

Major 7th shape

The barre chord shape for the major 7th chord with the root on the E string (illustrated previously), although being the most consistent with the other chord shapes, can be rather awkward to play clearly. The shape shown below may be preferred by some players and, whilst not strictly a barre chord, its use will be acceptable in the examination. Note that it is necessary to use the fretting-hand fingers to mute both the first and fifth strings in this shape.

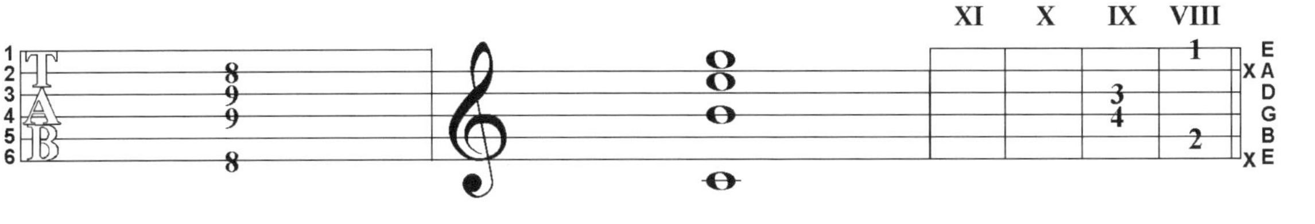

Rhythm playing

In this section of the examination, the candidate will be shown a chord chart and will be allowed a short time (of about 30 seconds) to study it before being asked to play it. The range of chords presented in the chord chart will be limited to the following:

- minor
- major
- minor 7th
- dominant 7th
- major 7th

After playing the first chord chart candidates may, at the examiner's discretion, be given an additional chart to play; this will be of similar difficulty to the first.

Some examples of the *type* of chart that may be presented at this grade are given below. The tempo markings are intended only as broad guidelines.

(i) Up tempo

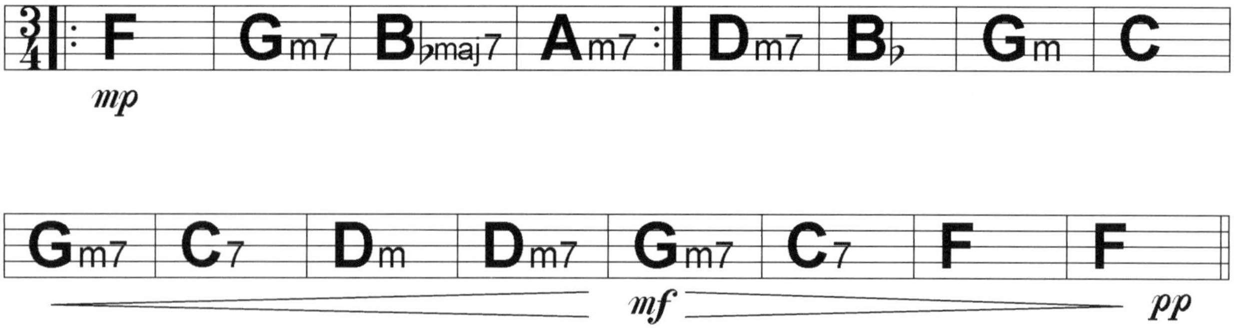

(ii) Bright and lively

(iii) Moderately slow

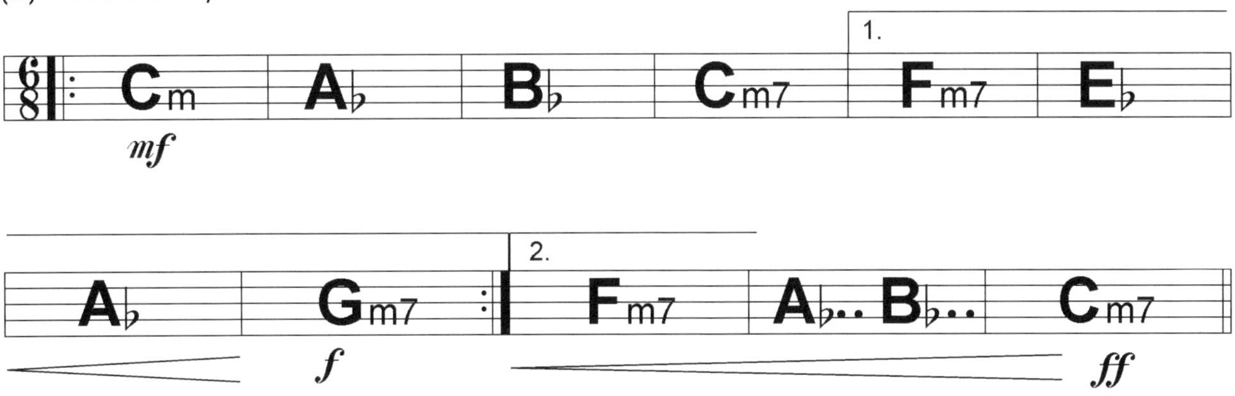

In practice, musicians may write out chord charts not only on staves (as shown previously) but sometimes chords are written above staves instead, or quite commonly just with bar lines (as in the example below). In the examination, to achieve maximum visual clarity, all chord charts will be presented in the style shown below.

(iv) Slowly

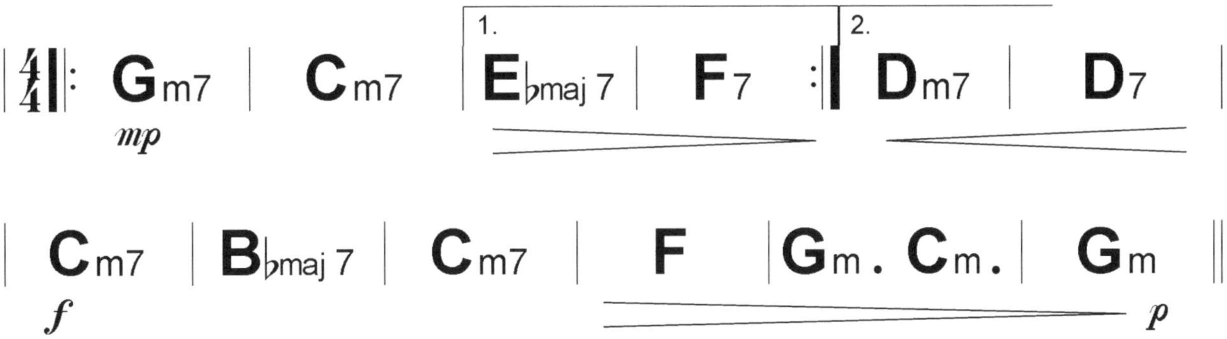

Split bars

When two (or more) chords appear in a single bar this is known as a split bar. Dots (or diagonal lines) after chords can be used to indicate the division of the bar: the chord symbol representing one beat and each dot representing another beat. If no dots are present it can be assumed that the bar is divided evenly between the chords.

INFORMATION AND ADVICE

At this grade the time signature is limited to either $\frac{3}{4}$, $\frac{4}{4}$ or $\frac{6}{8}$ time. Whilst the time signature should be evident by generally maintaining a regular pulse and even tempo, candidates are expected to be imaginative in their rhythm playing.

The musical style that is used is left to the discretion of the candidate. Fingerpicking can be used, rather than strumming, if preferred by the candidate.

Gaining marks

A maximum of 30 marks may be awarded in this section of the examination. The examiner will award marks for accuracy (including attention to time signature, repeats and dynamics), clarity, fluency and inventiveness.

Chords should ring clear, i.e. free of fret-buzz or the unintended muting of notes with the fretting-hand fingers. Chord changes should be as smooth and fluid as possible and lack any sense of hesitation. Care should be taken when choosing which barre shape to use (i.e. one based on the E string or one based on the A string) so that large fingerboard jumps between chords are avoided whenever possible.

During the time given to look over the chord chart, candidates should try to discover the overall structure of the progression. At this grade, the only indications on the chart, other than the time signature and tempo, are repeat and dynamic marks.

Repeat marks

Passages to be repeated are indicated by two vertical dots at the start and end of the section to be repeated. For example:

4/4 |: G | C :| D | G || should be played as:

4/4 | G | C | G | C | D | G ||

1st and 2nd time endings.

Bars marked 1. are included in the first playing, but omitted on the repeat playing and replaced with the bars marked 2. For example:

4/4 |: G | C | [1.] D | D7 :| [2.] B7 | Em || should be played as:

| G | C | D | D7 | G | C | B7 | Em ||

Dynamic markings

These indicate the graduations of volume.

ppp	*pp*	*p*	*mp*	*mf*	*f*	*ff*	*fff*
⇳		⇳		⇳			⇳
play as softly as possible		play softly		moderately loud			play as strongly as possible

< – become louder   > – become softer

RHYTHM PLAYING TIPS

Strumming hand

- It will aid fluency of rhythm playing if the strumming hand pivots from the wrist: a fluid and easy strumming action is best achieved this way, with the wrist loose and relaxed.

- If the wrist is stiff and not allowed to move freely then excessive arm movement will occur as the strumming action will be forced to come from the elbow instead. As this can never move as fluently as the wrist action there will be a loss of smoothness and rhythmic potential.

Fretting hand

- Be careful not to overgrip with the fretting-hand thumb on the back of the guitar neck as this will cause muscle fatigue and tend to limit the free movement of the thumb.

- It is essential that the fretting-hand thumb is allowed to move freely when changing chords. If the thumb remains static this restricts the optimum positioning of the fingers for the next chord, which may result in unnecessary stretching and the involuntary dampening of certain strings (as the fingers are not positioned upright on their tips).

- For the fingers to move freely, the wrist, elbow and shoulder must be flexible and relaxed: try to ensure that this is not inhibited by your standing or sitting position.

Lead playing

In this section of the examination, the candidate will be shown a chord progression containing chords chosen from those listed in Section 2 of this book. The examiner will then play this progression (either live or recorded) and the candidate should improvise over this using an appropriate scale selected from Section 1 of this book.

Some examples of the *type* of chord chart that will be presented at this grade are shown below. The scale suggestions are given for guidance in this book, but will NOT appear in the examination.

(i) The B♭ major scale could be used as the basis for improvising over the following progression...

B♭	B♭maj7	E♭maj7	E♭maj7	Dm	Dm7	Gm7	F7

(ii) The B pentatonic major scale could be used as the basis for improvising over the following progression...

B	G♯m7	G♯m7	F♯	B	D♯m7	D♯m7	Emaj7

(iii) The A♭ blues scale could be used as the basis for improvising over the following progression...

A♭7 . D♭7 .	A♭7 . E♭7 .	D♭7	A♭7	D♭7	E♭7

(iv) The B♭ natural minor scale could be used as the basis for improvising over the following progression...

B♭m	G♭maj7	G♭maj7	Fm7	E♭m7	B♭m7	G♭maj7	A♭

INFORMATION AND ADVICE

The progression will be played a total of four times; during the first playing the candidate should not play, but rather listen and digest the progression, before improvising over the next three cycles. After the final playing the progression will end on the key chord.

To ensure accuracy it is essential that the candidate selects the most appropriate scale with which to improvise. The examiner will NOT advise on this. At this grade each progression will always start on the key chord.

At the examiner's discretion an additional progression may be selected for the candidate to improvise over. Although this will again contain chords only from Section 2 of this book, the candidate may need to select a different scale from Section 1 to improvise with.

Gaining marks

A maximum of 30 marks may be awarded in this section of the examination. The examiner will award marks for:

- accuracy
- fluency
- phrasing and melodic shaping
- stylistic interpretation
- inventiveness and creativity
- clarity and tone production
- the application of specialist techniques

Although you will need to select a scale to improvise with, be aware that the purpose of the scale is only to set the series of notes that will be in tune in a particular key. Endeavour to make your improvisation melodically and rhythmically inventive and imaginative rather than sounding scale-like. The judicious use of movement and interplay between two different fingerboard positions for each scale will help in this objective.

The style of lead playing should enhance and empathise with the chordal accompaniment, which may be from a range of musical styles such as rock, pop, soul and blues etc. Try to create interesting melodic and rhythmic phrases within your improvisation and avoid inappropriate use of continuous scalic playing. Playing should be fluent, but without the need for speed for its own sake; more important is the overall musical effect that is achieved.

At this grade candidates are not expected to have a high level of fluency in the practical application of arpeggios, but the demonstration of some appropriate and accurate use of arpeggios during a performance will be reflected in the marks awarded.

SPECIALIST TECHNIQUES

At this grade, when musically appropriate, candidates should use of some of the following techniques during their improvisation:

String Bending

Candidates should be reasonably adept in executing ascending whole-tone bends, i.e. bending a note upwards by the equivalent of two frets. This is particularly useful for bending up to the octave from the ♭7th, or up to the 5th from the 4th.

Example taken from A Blues Scale:

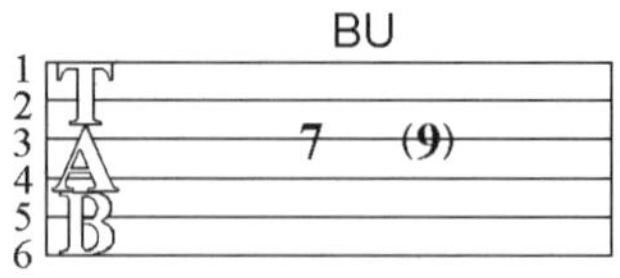

Bend D on the 7th fret, 3rd string, until it reaches the pitch of E – i.e. equivalent to playing on the 9th fret, 3rd string.

It is important to bend the string to exactly the right pitch. The pressure that is needed to bend a string will vary according to the string gauge and the fret position, so candidates will need to rely upon their aural abilities to pitch the note accurately. When bending a string with the third or fourth finger, keep the lower fingers on the string to give support and control. Using the power of the whole arm, pivoting from the elbow, will make string bending easier.

Vibrato

Vibrato is the wavering of the pitch of a note. It is differentiated from string bending in that the variation in pitch with vibrato is of a much smaller range. There are various methods by which vibrato can be executed whilst fretting a note:

(a) Horizontal vibrato: achieved by moving the fretting finger and hand from side to side whilst fretting a note.

(b) Vertical vibrato: achieved by moving the fretting finger vertically up and down to repeatedly shift the note slightly above pitch and back again.

(c) Wrist vibrato: whilst the first finger frets the note, the pitch of the note is altered with the rotation of the wrist.

Slurs

A slur is the sounding of two or more notes from the single pick of a string. Slurs can be used to facilitate fluency and speed, but equally importantly to add smoothness and subtlety. Candidates should be able to demonstrate ability with two types of slurs:

(a) *Hammer-on:* a note is played, then a higher note on the same string is sounded without being picked again but by a hammering action with a fretting-hand finger.

For the hammered note to be clear, it is important to use a certain amount of force and attack when bringing down the hammering finger.

Hammer with the tip of the finger as close to the fretwire as possible.

(b) *Pull-off:* fret a note and pick the string, then pull the fretting finger lightly downwards until it plucks the string and the lower note is sounded – i.e. without the string being picked again. If the lower note that is required is not an open string, then you need to have another finger in position fretting the lower note *before* executing the pull-off.

For the pull-off to be clear, it is important that the pressure is concentrated on the lower finger anchoring the string (otherwise the note may be pulled out of tune when the higher finger plucks the string).

The plucking action should come from the tip of the finger with a downward pulling action and not simply by lifting the finger off the string.

LEAD PLAYING TIPS

Phrasing

- Try to create interesting melodic and rhythmic phrases within your improvisation.
- Avoid the inappropriate use of continuous scalic playing by not being afraid to leave gaps between, and within, phrases.

Resolving notes

- When improvising from a scale you will find that some notes sound better, and more 'resolved', against certain chords than others. However, as long as you stay within the scale, no notes will be 'out of tune'. If you play a note that sounds 'unresolved' against a particular chord simply move up or down one note within the scale.
- Rest assured that none of the notes from the correct scale will totally clash with the backing chords; let your ears guide you as to which scale notes sound best over particular chords.

Interpretation

- Listen carefully to the chord progression and try to make your solo relate to the rhythm and style of the backing.

Spoken tests

A maximum of 10 marks may be awarded in this section of the examination.

FINGERBOARD KNOWLEDGE

In order to establish a solid musical foundation it is important that candidates should be aware of the notes that they are playing rather than merely duplicating finger patterns. At this grade, candidates will be expected to promptly name any note on any string, up to the 15th fret, as selected by the examiner.

Candidates may also be asked to name the notes contained within any of the required scales or arpeggios selected by the examiner.

During this section of the examination candidates will *not* be allowed to play the guitar to 'work-out' answers to this test.

CLARITY AND FLUENCY

Candidates may be asked questions about the optimum positioning of the fretting-hand fingers, in regard to achieving clarity and avoiding fret buzz. The most important factor being to press very close to the fretwire, and (except when holding a barre with the first finger) to use the tips rather than the pads of the fingers.

Candidates may also be asked questions about the optimum methods of achieving fluency when picking the strings. The most important factor being that plectrum strokes should generally alternate between down and up strokes in order to facilitate fluency and speed. Care should be taken to have an appropriate amount of plectrum tip protruding from the grip between the index finger and the thumb. Whilst this will vary with the size of fingers and the plectrum used, in general, too much plectrum showing will drag or even snag on the strings thus hampering fluency and articulation, whilst too little increases the chances of missing the correct string altogether.

KNOWLEDGE OF THE INSTRUMENT

Candidates should have knowledge of the ways in which the tone can be varied on their own instrument. This should include:

(i) A practical understanding of the use of tone controls and pick-up selectors (where appropriate).

(ii) An understanding of the effect of changing the right-hand position: playing at the bridge end generates the brightest tone, whilst movement towards the fingerboard tends to mellow the tone.

(iii) Knowledge of the effect of plectrum gauge and string gauge on tone production: a thicker plectrum and/or heavier strings can produce a fuller and more rounded tone than their lighter equivalents.

Candidates should have an understanding of the mechanism and anatomy of their guitar, including such terms as:

(i) *Action* – the distance between the strings and the frets, which determines the ease of fretting notes.

(ii) *Marker dots* (fret markers) – the dots, or blocks, inlaid into front and/or side of the fingerboard to act as a reminder as to the position of certain frets. These normally include at least frets 3, 5, 7, 9 and 12.

(iii) *The nut* – a slotted piece of material (normally plastic or brass), situated at the headstock end of the fingerboard, in the grooves of which the strings lie.

(iv) *The saddle* – the seat upon which the strings rest at the bridge end of the guitar. It is from this point that the vibrating section of the string starts. Electric guitars tend to have an individual saddle for each string, which form part of the bridge.

(v) *Machine Heads* – the turning keys, normally positioned on the guitar headstock, which when rotated increase or reduce string tension and so raise or lower the pitch of the string.

In addition, candidates should be able to explain the method they use to tune a guitar, and how to replace a string on their own instrument.

Aural assessments

A maximum of 10 marks may be awarded in total during this section of the examination. The candidate will be given a selection of the following tests, which will include a rhythm test and at least two other tests.

REPETITION OF RHYTHMS

The examiner will twice tap, or play (on a single note), a four bar rhythm in either $\frac{3}{4}$, $\frac{4}{4}$ or $\frac{6}{8}$ time. This may contain dotted quarter notes (doted crotchets), quarter notes (crotchets), eighth notes (quavers) and sixteenth notes (semiquavers) – except for the last bar, which will contain only one long note. The candidate should reproduce the rhythm by clapping, tapping or playing. Some examples of the *type* of rhythm are given below. Note that the first and third bars will be identical.

REPETITION OF MELODIC PHRASES

The candidate will be asked to look away while the examiner plays a one bar phrase in $\frac{4}{4}$ time. This will consist of notes, within a range of one octave, from a scale listed in Section 1 of this book. The candidate will be told which scale is to be used, and the keynote will be played. The phrase will start on the keynote and will consist of two quarter notes (crotchets) and four eighth notes (quavers).

The examiner will play the phrase twice before the candidate makes a first attempt to reproduce the phrase on the guitar. If required, the candidate can request the examiner to play the phrase one further time, prior to the candidate's second attempt, with no reduction in marks. However, the candidate will then be expected to reproduce the phrase promptly and will not be permitted any further attempts at 'working it out'. Some examples of the *type* of phrase are shown below.

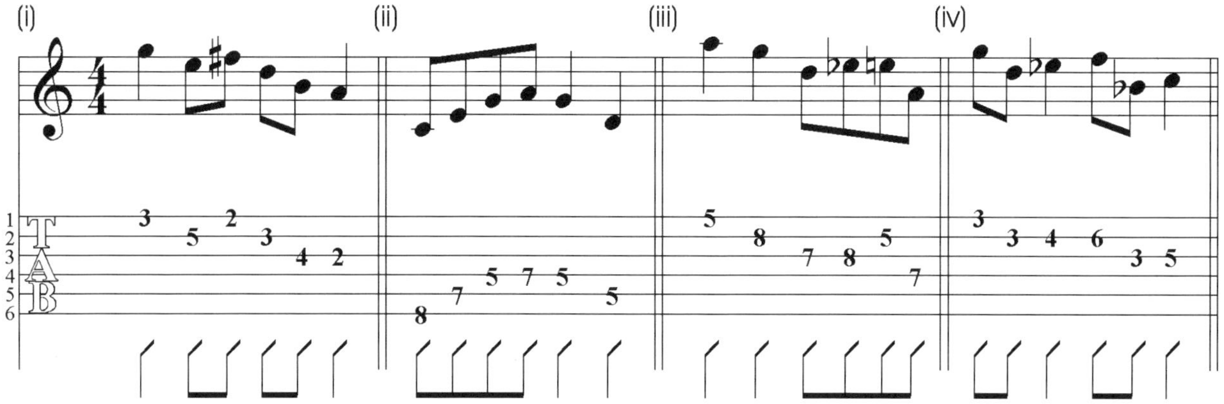

These phrases are taken from the following scales :
(i) G major, (ii) C pentatonic major, (iii) A blues, (iv) G natural minor.

KEEPING TIME

The examiner will twice play a four bar melody in either $\frac{3}{4}$, $\frac{4}{4}$ or $\frac{6}{8}$ time. After the first playing the candidate should identify the time signature. During the second playing the candidate should clap the main pulse, accenting the first beat of each bar. An example is given below, with the rhythmic pulse to be clapped by the candidate shown below both the notation and tablature.

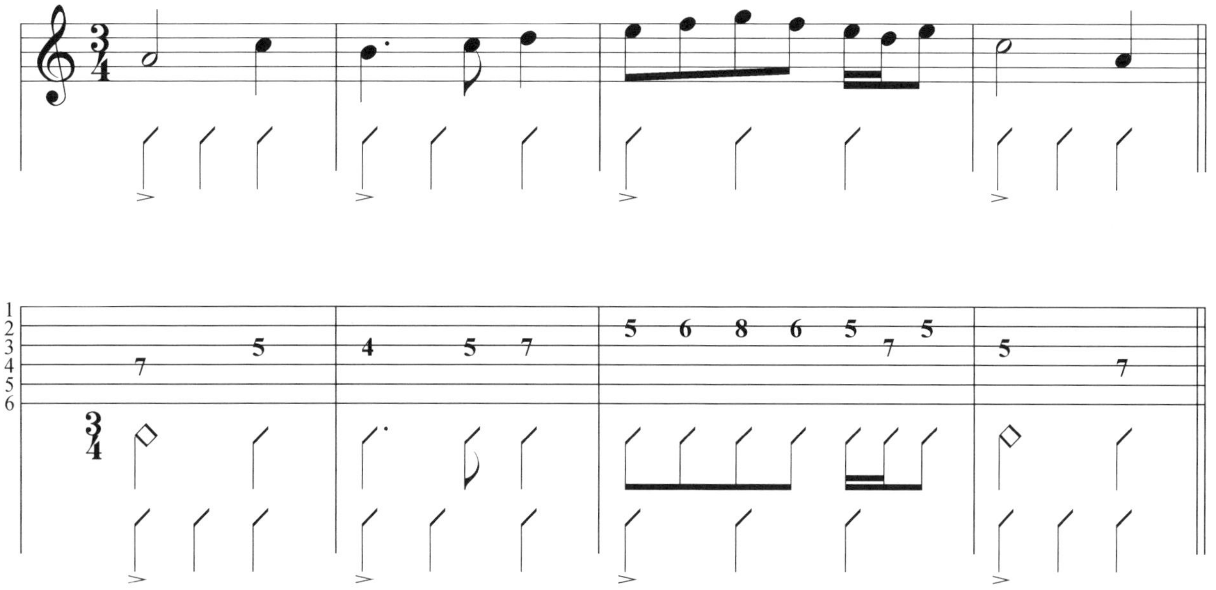

PITCH TEST

Whilst the candidate looks away the examiner will play an interval of a 3rd or a 7th in any key, sounding the notes separately. The candidate should identify whether the interval was major or minor. For example:

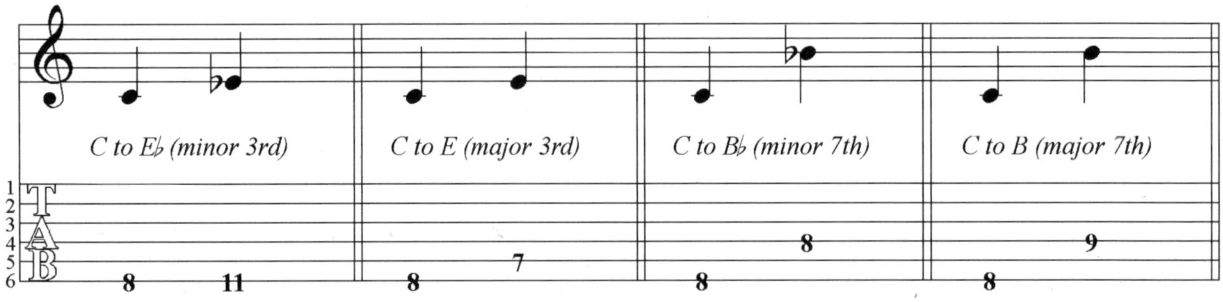

HARMONY TEST

Whilst the candidate looks away the examiner will twice strum either a minor 7th, dominant 7th or major 7th chord. The candidate will then be asked to identify the type of chord that was played.